G-Tube Feeding By

A Busy Mom

The Tale Of How I Fed

My Child To Victory

By Jessica L Valentini

ISBN 13: 978-1480055087

ISBN 10: 1480055085

This book is for educational purposes. It is not intended as a substitute for medical advice. Please consult a qualified health care professional for individual health and medical advice. Author shall not have any responsibility for any adverse effects arising directly or indirectly as a result of the information provided in this book.

Table of Contents

∞Disclaimer ∞

This book is not a medical diagnosis or to be used as such. Before changing any diet, especially your special needs child, talk to your doctor or other qualified healthcare providers to ensure the best course of action for your child's individual needs.

~ Introduction ~

Sometimes it seems like a lot of people with testimonials or self-help guides don't really tell you how they did it. I hope you will agree with me that this is not one of those books. Like you, I was a parent who was looking for answers to ease my little one's feeding pains. What I found was that not only was my little guy happier, but that making his food put joy back into mealtime for all of us.

I would like to point out that I am not a doctor, or even a medical professional. I am an accountant turned stay-at-home mother of two who has studied nutrition as a hobby for over 10 years. This book is not intended for a replacement to the advice or guidance given by qualified healthcare professionals. It is more of a personal testimony of how I decided to take my g-tube fed child off of pre-made formula. I have included some advice and tips to avoid my most common mistakes.

My intent for this book is to help you avoid mistakes I made and give you a few references on where and how you can keep learning about different topics for your family's overall health. Moreover, I want to give you the confidence to open dialogue with your doctor or find another if it doesn't seem like they have your child's best interest at heart. You will find that most doctors are not a fan of making your own food because of malnourishment concern for your child. Also, most have general fear instilled in them by the drug and healthcare systems currently in place with skewed research results to convince us that the risky way is the only way.

Don't let the arrogance of an over confident doctor override the love and care of a good parent who has to live with the decisions made about the child's well-being. There are good doctors and other healthcare professionals that are great at what they do and will give you the tools and support needed for this journey.

This book is short, but to the point. I have never been one to beat around the bush, as it is said. And your time is precious. So let's get going!

Chapter 1

~ WHY I DID IT ~

I would like to say that I am not against pre-made formulas as a whole because my child would not have made it this far without it. But it does not seem to be something that should be a way of life if it doesn't need to be.

My son seemed to be growing at a normal rate while he was on the doctor's recommended pre-made formula diet. However, it was not covered by our medical insurance. At $180 per case of food, it would have cost about $360 for him to eat for a month. We were fortunate enough to find people who had a surplus of this food with a more affordable price. And a sympathetic pediatrician's office who knew we were going through a tough time financially and emotionally.

Despite mixing extra water and sometimes some stage 1 baby food into the formula, it did not ease the reflux that he seemed to have while on formula. Changing formulas until it was "hypo-allergenic" and even dairy free did not help. Medicine was not helping either. We tried at least three different prescriptions, compounded for him just for reflux. We found that after a few months, the prescriptions were not easing his discomfort. We even tried a medicine that would make the muscles contract in the esophagus to try to keep the food and acid from traveling up from the stomach. Short of surgery, we were not given other options in hope of easing his misery.

The constant vomiting was more than I thought I could mentally bear. It made everyone's lives miserably, his especially. Not only was this hindering him from being happy, he was left with this formula as the choice of liquid to take orally. He slowly became disinterested in using a bottle until he got to a point of refusal. How could I blame him? If it didn't taste good coming up, why would anyone choose to swallow it down into their body?

I kept thinking to myself, there has got to be a better way to help him, but how? The doctor's kept insisting on the food that we could barely afford. No one in our family was happy. Frustration and burn out both mentally and physically were taking its toll on our family as well. Vomiting occurred in the middle of the night, during the day, the first feed and everywhere else in between. It happened at home, in the car, or in a store. It kept us from sleeping normally at night. It was a free for all where no one was winning. It was to a point where we could not trust or find someone to watch our children because of the level of difficulty his care seemed to be in comparison to a "well child".

Our gastrointestinal doctor was known for getting kids to eat on their own through various types of therapy. However, she did not support a parent veering away from "The Formula", as their source of food. Without the support of my GI doctor, I decided to start my journey. I looked online to research what other parents were doing in hopes of finding support to work towards this goal. Most were as clueless as I was about how to begin. What seemed worse were the parents who did find a way but were promoting the use of mixers that cost hundreds of dollars. And a lot were making recipes that sounded very unappetizing and full of more expensive ingredients. If I did this, I knew that I would have to do it on my own with foods that I could feed everyone in the family. And I would do it with the limited but reliable kitchen equipment that I already owned. And it has been the best decision for my son and our family!

Chapter 2

~ The Plan.....Goes Out the Window ~

So I thought my plan was simple. I would replace a few of his foods with some premade liquid foods such as soups or bisques. It would be as organic and wholesome as I could afford. Unfortunately, a very large volume of soup would have to be given and still fail at providing a whole day's need of calories and nutrients, let alone one meal. Now let me say that soups are a great source of quick foods in a pinch, but it will not meet all of the protein needs for your child. But those soups gave me the hope that I needed. I would just have to add more food to it to build up the nutrition.

Roasted Red Pepper and Tomato soup or Butternut Squash soups were my favorites, so I started out using what I thought taste good. It was thin enough to go through the tube straight out of the carton. I started with replacing one or two meals a day with it. I wanted to make sure he responded to other foods well. He did, however I needed more nutrients for him if he was going to thrive on food I made full-time. I asked myself, "What kind of foods would he be eating right now at his age? What kind of foods do I like to eat?" By asking myself those two questions, it led me to the base recipes I created, and you will find at the end of this book. I used ingredients such as Greek yogurt, a super food power formulated for kids, coconut oil, almond butter, baby food, juice, bananas, apples and other seasonal fruit along with almond milk, coconut milk, and eggs. You will not find all of these ingredients in the recipes given, but you should be able to use it to suit your own tastes and recipes.

I would like to point out that nut based items should not be introduced to children under the age of two. Please talk to your pediatrician or health care provider about the recommended ages to introduce foods such as dairy, nuts, honey and fish to their diet. If you have any concerns for some of these ingredients because of allergies, look into the alternative items. Butter from sunflower seeds may meet your needs and has a decent amount of protein per serving. Soy is not something I suggest for boys, as it is known to increase estrogen levels when eaten in large amounts regularly. Not to mention it is usually a Genetically Modified Organism, or GMO as it is referred to on food labels.

Each person enjoys different foods, so please use my experience as an inspiration to think of foods that suit your family, your child, and your child's medical needs. I have been blessed with a child that does not have food allergies and was able to feed him a variety of foods. However, if you have concerns about specific food allergies, it is possible to have preliminary testing performed to avoid possible reactions to foods, pollen and other allergens.

I hope that was enough information to convince you that you can do this for your child. You can start introducing and eventually feeding him or her real, whole, and even delicious food. Moreover, I hope this is enough information to encourage and convince you to seek medical advice before starting this process, especially if there are concerns or a history of food allergies for your child or other family members.

Chapter 3

~ Let's Get Down To Business ~

Now that we have covered a little bit of my background, and made sure that the lawyers and doctors are happy, let's get down to business. I have found that I can make my child food that is good for him, that tastes good, and that eventually developed into even more encouragement for him to start eating his foods orally.

Why do I believe it led him to more oral feedings? I started observing my son's behavior before, during and after a tube feeding. He was burping, sometimes right in my face after his feed. I realized a simple truth known to all. You usually taste your food in a burp. Despite the use of the g-tube bypassing his mouth, he still tasted the food being put into his body. Just like we may burp up "flavors" after a meal, it brings to memory a good or bad experience.

It seems even the most common sense of behaviors is overlooked when you have a child with special needs. My son does not currently communicate the same way I do with a voice and articulated words. And he does not eat the same way I do through my mouth. It does mean that his body can have the same reaction to food as I do. It also means to have healthy brain development and to become more intelligent, he needs mental stimulation to learn and stay mentally sharp and focused. His body also requires healthy fats, proteins, carbohydrates, fluids and exercise just like my body needs.

The only variable in this equation is the path used to administer the nutrients needed for a properly functioning body. So what is the plan? What is your child's equation of nutrition? Well hopefully by the end of this book you will know, and have a plan of action. Again, talk with your health care providers. Chances are your GI has a nutritionist available that can tell you the guidelines of nutrition your child needs. You need information such as daily caloric intake, grams of protein, fiber and sugar. Levels of sodium and the amount of hydration needed in a day are also important, as well as the specific dietary needs your child requires in his or her situation as some medications deplete vitamins and minerals our body needs.

 Don't be shy if you are serious about changing your child's diet. If you start asking questions but find your doctor not being forthright in giving you the information or tools needed to do this, you may want to consider hiring another doctor. (I will rant a little more on this later.) You and your doctor should be a team, not a dictatorship.

Once you have the numbers you need, create a chart. Log what your child eats at every feed. This may seem a little tedious, but it is the only way to plan and track their progress. I even make notations as to when bowel movements are and size. This has helped me determine constipation and what foods work to "keep things moving" without the aid of over the counter medications. I preferred tracking these items in a chart that counts down what was given so I always knew what I had left to administer instead of performing a math problem after each meal.

There is no wrong way to track it, so long as it is tracked. Eventually it will become second nature. If you find that you are struggling to make the numbers work, sit down and plan out (if you have not already) the daily and maybe even weekly meal plan. It will save you time and probably a few extra trips to the grocery store.

The best course is a planned course when it comes to this new lifestyle. Planning ahead and spending a few extra minutes in the kitchen a few times a week prepping foods will help when time seems short or unexpected plans start to take over your day. The peace of mind that your little one has food ready to go will make this the desirable, stress free way of life you may be looking for as a reality.

Chapter 4

~ Tools of the Trade ~

When I first started looking into feeding my son real food, I noticed a trend. Everyone was using a very expensive blender. Now don't get discouraged. I'm not suggesting you spend $200-$450 dollars on a new blender. I probably would have bought one had I the money to do so at the time. Especially considering the stories I heard from one woman about the constant burn out of ordinary blenders used grinding up meats and other tough foods for her mother who was on a feeding tube.

Well I can tell you that it is possible to do without the heavy artillery. If you already have a big blender, great it can be used. If not, do not despair. You are still going to make healthy foods for your child. Here are your tools of the trade, which I suspect you may have already in your kitchen.

Food Processor-Mix and puree most of the meals in this wonderful machine to ensure a thin consistency needed to go through the tube and button. Depending on the size and brand you should be able to find one between $15-$100.

Whisks-I use a small whisk to blend foods which are already pureed. Especially if it is late at night and I don't want to wake the house. I prefer using a larger whisk for the custard base I use as a source of protein. The average price is between $3 - $8 each.

Potato Masher- There is a few different varieties of these magical manual kitchen tools. I personally prefer the one that has the metal squiggle in the middle just like mom used. This thing is great. I use it to mash up bananas, cooked carrots, and other cooked fruits and vegetables. It cuts down on the use of the motor, and produces a product that can be liquid-like in the food processor when blended. The average price is between $5-$15 each.

Fine Mesh Strainer-This is a must have tool. Used to strain any and possibly all foods you make to ensure blockages in the feeding tube system are avoided. Items that may cause blockage are foods that may not blend well such as blended hard boiled eggs, seeds and skins from fruits or any other lump that may not be immediately visible to the naked eye. The average price is between $3-$10.

Measuring Cups and Spoons-Proper measuring cups and spoons are necessary to ensure consistency of recipes and determine caloric intake of items put into your recipe. The average price is between $2-$10 each.

Storage Containers and Lids-Various sizes will be needed to keep bulk protein mixes or extra foods prepped ahead of time. Make sure it has a good seal to ensure freshness and safe food handling practices. The average price varies.

I have found that these simple tools were all I needed to provide my child with the nutrients he required whether at home or on the go. Best of all, each has a use in an everyday kitchen setting to maximize any investment you make.

I know not everyone has a food processor. Before you decide you don't need one or cannot afford a large machine right now, let me convince you otherwise. This tool is great as it can be versatile for other uses. Some come as an attachment to use on standard blender platforms. A few models have extra blades that slice, dice and shred.

A great resource for finding a good price on a reliable brand would be closeout stores or specialty kitchen stores in outlet malls. Buy the size you feel comfortable using and that fits your wallet. With that said, I will tell you that I made all of my child's meals with a small electric food chopper or food processor (depending on who is in the kitchen). It has a capacity of three to four cups of liquid. I usually mixed the actual meals together one at a time as needed. There were a few times a larger capacity container would have been helpful. But it was not inconvenient enough to prompt the purchase of a larger capacity machine.

If you are not sure what size will fit your needs, consider asking to borrow a machine from someone you know who already owns one. Most people do not use it on a daily basis and won't miss it during your trial run.

Now you are armed and ready to start cooking!

Chapter 5

~ The Basics ~

Here are a few basics on what you should know about proteins, fats and carbohydrates. Each has a function that works together. The fats help absorb the vitamins and nutrients and are good for the body and the brain. Some of which are absorbed from our carbohydrates and proteins. Healthy proteins eaten with healthy simple carbohydrates slow down the processing of the carbohydrates and maintain a more stable blood sugar level.

Protein intake is important for our little one's development. I try to feed him lean proteins, but try not to allow worries of cholesterol hinder the choices. More than likely your child does not have cholesterol issues, so using eggs everyday should not be a concern. A quality egg is a great source of protein as well as vitamins and minerals. It is also easy on the pocket book.

Protein takes longer for the body to process. Regular protein throughout the day served with fruits and vegetables will help keep blood sugar levels steady and enable a routine eating schedule to follow daily.

Protein is very important for healthy growth and development. Do be mindful of giving your child protein in very high quantities at one time. Too much protein in a diet puts a strain on kidney functions. Synthetic or condensed proteins like you might find in protein bars or protein shakes should be avoided as excessive use will take a toll on the kidneys over time.

If you do need to use a protein supplement, consider egg white based supplements. Now, I have not tried this yet. So why tell you about it? Because I do not know your child's specific needs, and I want you to have viable options to look at that you may not be aware of otherwise. This product seems more of a challenge to locate in a store, but a good quality powder might be a great staple to have in your cupboards on those days or mornings you are short on time. Again, real sources of proteins found in nature such as lean meat, fish, and poultry, legumes, nuts, eggs, pseudo grains, yogurt and cheese products are always the best choice for your body.

Pseudo grains such as quinoa and amaranth have a great source of protein as well as overall nutrients. The only problem I have with it its ability to be broken down in some of the blenders and choppers.

Cook up a batch and see if it is a contender as one of your staples. Usually you cook it 1 measurement of grain to 5 measurements of water. So one cup of dried quinoa to 5 cups of water usually cooks it well. Try a tablespoon of cooked quinoa ground in water. If you cannot get it to grind up fine enough to push through a tube, discard it as the risk of clogging the tube system is too great. Eat the leftovers with some thawing berries from the freezer section, and you have breakfast for other members of the family.

If you want to learn more about protein, fat and carbohydrates, and how all of these things work together, I suggest reading the South Beach Diet Book by Dr. Arthur Agatston. This book explains the process of the body and how it uses food in a format that is easy to understand. The diet is not for children and should not be looked at as such, but the natural process of the body is for all.

Chapter 6

~ Let's Talk Extras ~

We have talked about basic needs; let's talk about how to build up foods to meet your child's needs.

Let's start with powdered supplements. In addition to fresh foods in your child's diet, you may consider super food supplement powders to give some meals an extra punch of vitamins and minerals. There are some great products on the market today geared directly towards kids to ensure easy absorption. Some even have great berry flavor if you want to encourage oral intake.

I suggest mixing the powder in yogurt or any other food mixture you are using in which the flavors complement one another. Some labels suggest mixing the powder in juice or water. If you decide to do that for your g-tube fed child, know that the super food powders do not easily dissolve. I have found it likes to settle in a clump and clog the syringe, or even the line of the feeding bag. Even the button entry into the stomach can become clogged when mixed in straight liquid. Moreover, if you are feeding it orally to any child, the floating fiber may turn them off from trying it all together.

The powders are a great way to add real nutrients and calories to a feed or a smoothie without adding the heaviness of another food to increase the volume needed to meet the caloric and nutritional daily intake. You can find this kind of product in your local health store and even in the baby food isle at the local grocery store as individual packages.

Fat and vitamins do have a healthy relationship. I know fat has gotten a bad name because of all the processed man-made foods on the market today. Do not regard healthy fat as an unnecessary addition to your child's diet. Healthy fat which you find in nuts, lean protein and fish are necessary for healthy brain function as well as nutrients absorption in the digestive system.

Good sources of healthy fats are found in coconut and virgin cold expelled coconut oil, avocado or avocado oil, olive oil, fish and even fish oils. Watch for added Trans Fats or blended oils which may have canola or other less healthy oils added to it.

If your little one suffers from constipation you may even consider flax seed oil to introduce extra fiber. In my opinion, it does not seem necessary to use flax seed oil and fish oil at the same time as similar benefits are found in both. It is more of a personal preference as to which you want to use. Remember, you should not use oils excessively as it is higher in calories but not an all-around nutritional meal on its own.

Vitamins and minerals are important to every living person and plant on this Earth. But each person has a unique composition and may need a little more or a little less of one. If you are not sure, and have specific concerns, testing for low amounts of B's and D's is becoming more common. Overall, unless your child has severe health concerns, a multivitamin is usually an easy and effective way to ensure your child's body is receiving what it needs.

Multi-vitamins come in a lot of different forms now, including liquid for infants all the way to adults. Please make sure you are using one that is appropriate for your child's age as too much of some vitamins are dangerous to the body. As with everything else, moderation is a key to success. It is recommended by most qualified healthcare professionals that you do not take multi-vitamins on a continual basis to avoid ineffectiveness of the vitamin as well as avoiding buildup of some vitamins that the body may not use as quickly.

My general rule of thumb for this is once a bottle of the multi-vitamin is empty. I wait 2-4 weeks before replacing it. Instead of replacing it with another vitamin, I switch over to a fish oil supplement for my child. When the fish oil supplement is gone, I wait 2-4 weeks and purchase the multi-vitamin again. This method has made it simple for me to follow what I am giving my child and somehow put me in line with the sale of these products at my local warehouse store. Fish oil products are even available for children in gummy form where vitamins are sold. If oral intake is possible for any of your children, this is another great option.

If you are unsure of which kind of fish oil to buy I suggest you consider krill oil. Krill oil seems to be all the rage right now as it has the highest content of Omega-3 than any other fish oil. But don't just take my word for it, do your research on this and the other supplements that are available at your local store. Not all supplements and oils are created equally. Be aware of Trans Fats and MSG ingredients that are not healthy but still added to some products.

Finally, probiotics are becoming more main stream and doctors are recognizing the need for it to be added to daily diets. The probiotics build up all the good bacteria that have most likely been destroyed by taking antibiotics. If your little one is sick a lot and antibiotics were needed for them whether in the womb or any other time in their life, they probably need a good probiotic to build up their immune system again.

Not all probiotics are created equal. Never give your child a probiotic product made for adults. Children under 2 are especially at risk if given a probiotic not designed specifically for their age. The wrong probiotic can bore holes in your child's intestines, need I say more? Please talk to your pediatrician to see if they have a brand to recommend. My pediatrician was very supportive and was the one to first suggest the use of probiotics for our little one.

I know some stipulations have been made suggesting probiotics irritate the skin around the g-tube button because of stomach acid. So be mindful of that when introducing it to your child's diet. There are powder probiotics made specifically for young children. If your child shows signs of irritation around the g-tube consider reducing how much is given at one time. Break down the dose into 2 or more doses throughout the day. Just like vitamins, your child shouldn't need a probiotic year round. Again, talk to your pediatrician to assist you in using a probiotic for your child. A good rule of thumb would be 4-6 weeks on and 2 months off if your child does not receive a lot of antibiotics regularly. The product label should give you a good indication of how their product is administered and expected to be used to get the most out of the product.

Chapter 7

~ The Results ~

So, what happened when I applied this knowledge, and switched my child to real food? Here is what happened and why I believe it to be.

The Beginning

First of all, I must point out that a lot of prayer has been performed by me and others to God, as it is not His Will for anyone to be ill. This is why I believe my son progressed so quickly. But it was revealed to me how this helped him, so I would like to share it with you.

Before I changed my son's diet, vomiting every day, approximately 1-3 times on average, was a common occurrence. He would not drink from a bottle or special cups, nor eat very much food by mouth, if at all, on a regular basis. I was frustrated because I wanted my child to succeed but wasn't sure how to help him. Feeding time was dreaded, and the constant changing of sheets and clothing on all involved would produce an overwhelming amount of laundry. Going out on daily excursions would be filled with anxiety: did I pack enough food, extra clothing, is the pump charged enough?

The experts meant well, but it seemed that any idea outside their basic training they were not willing to explore or acknowledge. It was too risky if it didn't fit into the box they called their field. But they didn't have to live every day with their advice given by them as fact. So I knew if my son was going to improve I was going to have to do something they were not comfortable with me doing. But as his parent, I had the right to do what is best for my child.

Looking back I'm glad I did it. I wish I had the courage to do it sooner instead of living in constant fear of "the system". It is unfortunate that this system has forced a lot of parents into it because there was no alternative. A system that deems you bad or unfit because you dare to challenge the status quo, going above and beyond to seek truth to improve your child's quality of life. With that said, please do what you can to find a doctor or doctors and therapists who will work with you and support you. Stop wasting your time with doctors and therapists who do not have consideration and respect for you or your child. Your child deserves to have every option you can provide available to him or her. And you and your family deserve to have the best quality of life possible together.

The Result

During the first two months my son was taken completely off of the formula I saw immediate results. He was happier when he woke up. He was happier during the day and even happy at night (before he got tired). He went from being sick with reflux all the time to no reflux at all. The vomiting completely stopped as if I flipped a switch. I started to have courage to try feeding him by mouth again. He went from not eating anything by mouth to eating at least 80% of his daily needs. It was amazing to say the least.

This is why I believe it worked. No longer was the same horrible taste going in and coming out of his body. But instead the variety of food going in was finally a positive experience for him. He was feeling better and acting happier overall. He had regular bowel movements after about 1-2 weeks without the aid of an over the counter stool softener. And he was enjoying the flavors he burped up so much, he was willing to eat, and excited to do it.

Overall the experience has had a great impact on our family. Eating and feedings are no longer viewed as a fearful chore knowing it will create unhappiness for our son. Extended family members are becoming more confident in their ability to help or just be involved with him. And our faith in God has grown. He can only do what we believe He can do, so is the gift of Free Will.

Now I know that everyone has a unique situation to deal with that may not have as quick of a result as I have seen. However, the most important point is to do what is best for your child to grow and develop.

One other point I would like to make is about therapy, as it did play a role in all of this. A speech therapist once told us that crawling and eating go hand in hand in a child's development. Is that true? I am not sure. Our son was not doing either. I found a book written by Dr. Glenn Dolman, who shed a lot of light on what our son needed as well as confirmed feelings I had about some suggested therapies for our son's care. I encourage any parent who is looking for the healing solutions to their child's hindrances to read his book. You will find it along with other resources of interest in the Appendix.

Once we started doing the suggested patterning in this book to encourage crawling, our son started to root for food again. I used it as my second cue to try his oral feedings, and he has been progressing ever since.

Now this book and the institute's practices have a lot of mixed reviews about it in the medical field. But I can say that we started to see improvement with suggested patterning. And a lot of the measurements used by all pediatric caregivers have been based off of the benchmarking system they created. You will notice that what traditional therapists do mimics at least one thing that was created out by this institute. It is amazing how the medical community band together to fight untraditional options that they are willing to "borrow ideas" from as their own.

Your child should be able to find their level of success just as much as any other child. At least, give them the chance to try. If I had not allowed my child this opportunity, we would still be scrubbing carpets instead of hearing his new found voice of laughter.

Chapter 8

~ His Menu ~

Now the foods I chose to feed my son were everyday foods that a small child his age would normally eat. I just had to determine how to make it small enough to get through his tube. Eggs, yogurt, "sandwich" with nut butter, milk, juice and bananas would be my main staples. Those were the simple foods my first born loved to eat, so why would the second one be much different (my mental reasoning)? Are there foods you remember or your parents said you enjoyed eating at a young age? Chances are your child will enjoy it also.

Now remember we talked about the importance of protein in an earlier chapter. My goal was to focus on the protein requirement first, and the calories second. Your priority needs to fit your child's dietary and developmental needs. Nevertheless, everyone needs a starting point, and that was mine.

Here is the list of staples I kept on hand:

- ➢ All Natural Creamy Roasted Almond Butter
- ➢ Eggs
- ➢ Unsweetened Almond Milk
- ➢ Unsweetened Almond and Coconut Milk Blend
- ➢ Plain Greek Yogurt
- ➢ Organic Low Sodium Chicken Broth
- ➢ Stage 1 Jar, Meat Only Baby Food
- ➢ Stage 2 Pureed Fruit Baby Food
- ➢ Bananas
- ➢ Apple Juice
- ➢ Coconut Oil

Most of the items listed would be used in a base or thinning agent to create a meal for my son. Most of it was in a quick use stage so I could make food fast and yet it was food that other people in the family already ate.

 A few of these items may seem or sound expensive. It can be if you are limited in store options. I was able to save a lot of money on these items, some 50% savings, by shopping at a large warehouse store. My preference is Costco because they have the same price on the majority of my staple items in Arizona as well as Michigan (which I travel between every year). If you cannot get your own membership, chances are you know at least one person who does and is more than happy to help you obtain these items.

Chapter 9

~ The Biggest Challenge ~

When you first start your journey to replace formula meals with your homemade meals, you are going to have to adjust your thinking. The required calories per feeding could be a higher or lower volume of liquid as a whole than what your child received on formula. This will change the time frame in which you may have fed your child by pump. Moreover, it could change the need of extra liquid per day that you have to give him or her.

You also need to be aware that some foods pureed may not break down the way you may expect. I do not recommend most of these items to be administered through an automated pump as it will require a greater degree of thinning verses using a feeding syringe. Items such as raspberries, strawberries and blueberries have a lot of seeds and do not fit through the button. Hard boiled eggs tend to get too gritty and clog up the line and button as well. (Straining is important but may not catch everything if your strainer does not have a fine mesh.)

I tried to mirror the formula's calories per ounce the best I could to use as a blueprint of how much he was receiving in calories, protein, fat, vitamins, fiber and everything else pertinent to his health. This plan, if you will, can give you the basic guidelines for creating your own recipes and a foundation to have a dialogue with your nutritionist or other healthcare provider.

The biggest challenge and very important task to perform is tracking your child's food, including the calories, protein and liquids along with the foods names to ensure enough nutrition is received and dehydration does not occur. This might be a little tedious when you begin, but if your child does great or does not do well on a particular food, it will be captured here so a quick solution can be found.

Chapter 10

~ Time-Friend or Foe ~

Making food constantly and blending every meal is sometimes a daunting thought. Using foods that you have made for the entire family is ideal. For days that have decided to veer from the plan, have staples on hand for quick meal emergencies.

When you make dinner, make extra carrots, potatoes, squash, or any other soft cooked vegetable without butter to mash and blend. Using vegetables and starches you are making for the rest of the family will cut down on prep time, and can be added to your protein base. Moreover, it will help incorporate your child into mealtimes and promote more togetherness and sense of belonging. Don't overlook the use of fish in your child's diet when cooked for the whole family. Mashed with a fork and then put in the food processor with liquid and vegetable. Easy to make and is easy on the machine as well. Best of all it is a great addition to your child's meal plan.

Turn Around an Oops with Soups! Didn't have time to make a base? Soups and broths are nice to have for a light snack or to use as a base. If it is something you like to use as a base, consider purchasing soups in cardboard containers that can be opened and closed easily for multi-day uses. Try to avoid high sodium items and items that may have noodles or other chunky foods as it may not blend smooth enough to fit through the tube. Boxed soups can also be stored unopened for a while to keep for emergency situations. Especially important if you live in an area of power outages during winter months and tornado season. Always check your use by dates and rotate your staples accordingly as you would any other food in your pantry or emergency kit.

Baby food is another great option for on the fly meals and to keep on hand in case of power outages. Already premeasured, pureed and a nutritional label to log into your meal sheet, it is a great option and my go to staple in a pinch. Best of all, it will keep for a few months without preservatives. Used with a premade base and a whisk and you will be whipping up your child's meal with ease. I prefer the stage two baby foods as it is pureed enough to use anytime. The wide selection of food combinations is ideal should your child not like some of the flerps (flavor burps) produced.

A great protein in a pinch is also found in the baby food isle. Some of the first stage meat with broth jars of baby food can contain as much as 10 grams of protein. It can be a great source to use on a regular basis in the meals you fix for your child. I have found that the meat only baby foods still require a little grind in the food processor because of the meat fibers. I do not advise putting it or any food made through the tube without straining it through a semi-fine to fine mesh strainer. It is a prudent practice to have a trial run through a tube used for such verification on any new recipe you use. This should reduce your chances of clogging up your child's tube and button. A bonus to using jarred baby food meat means less ware on your machine, prolonging its useful life. Moreover, if you are having chicken, beef or turkey, your child can also have it just like the rest of the family.

Chapter 11

~Behavior Issues or Nutrition~

There seems to be more and more research on nutrition and its effects on behavior. Children with special dietary or behavioral needs may find great success on a more natural diet. I would like to state again, I do not have ill will towards companies producing formulas that deliver sustenance when conventional ways are not possible. But foods that are man-made are usually not the best choice for long term health and development.

Nothing that is man-made can be better for our bodies than natural whole foods in the long run. Omitting items with dyes and other seemingly harmless chemicals have been known to improve a child's behavior. This can be true for gluten and dairy intolerance as well. Although I cannot confirm this as fact, it makes me wonder if more foods create allergic reactions disguised as bad behavior. What other ailments are masks for poor behavior and learning hindrances? I have witnessed a child diagnosed with ADHD by a child physiatrist and then diagnosed by another health care professional as infected tonsils which has the same behavior effects. Who knew? Thank God for science that we know even this much, and that the boy had a mother who got a second opinion before drugging her child unnecessarily!

You may notice that I do not mention foods that are soy, rice, corn, peanut, or wheat based. Well, I have a good reason for that. There is a lot of research that has been done in this country, as well as others that is not well known, yet. Some foods are linked to fungus, which can produce micro toxins in our bodies creating a whole list of troubles and illnesses the majority of the medical professionals believed only drugs can help. Some even masked as cancer. If your child has diabetes or cancer or any other ailment, I would encourage you to do research and read The Fungus Link by Doug Kaufmann. His books along with his show Know The Cause educate, but also sites resources that are valuable. This platform with its mix of credible guests may have the answer you are seeking.

If you want to learn more about formula and what doesn't have to be told to the public, subscribe to Dr. Mercola's website. He is a real doctor with a heart for nutrition. It is a nice resource to have from a person who does not go to "extremes" and looks for innovation instead of criticizing it. Moreover, I personally like his straightforward information that is easy to understand. Dr. Mercola and Doug Kaufmann's information can be found with other valuable resources at the end of this book.

Chapter 12

~ Final Advice ~

In closing, I would like to wish you well in your new journey to bring your child to a higher quality of life. I realize that some of this information may be new and unfamiliar to most. Some may even call it radical or extreme. I implore you to keep an open mind and an open dialogue with your child's health care providers. More importantly, do not just take my word or anyone's word as absolute. Verify the information on your own. A little research on your end might produce the right question or even the answer you didn't realize you needed to seek.

You know your child better than any doctor, so take their advice and relate it to your child. There is always a viable solution that will benefit your child. If something doesn't feel right, say something right away. Remember, you and your healthcare providers are supposed to be on the same team, not opposing where the child usually loses.

Keep moving forward and don't look at any hiccups as a failure. Just like Thomas Edison who would not claim failure, but instead "discovered 999 ways how not to make a light bulb." My prayer is that every family who reads this book finds success and healing, as God's Will has always been for us to be happy and well.

Chapter 13

~ Recipes ~

Here are some basic recipes I used to help get you started. Remember I was able to make all of these recipes with small inexpensive kitchen tools. I did not include the caloric information. Make sure that as you add to these recipes that you write down all of your measurements. Put it through the recipe analyzer at www.caloriecounter.com. A great resource I found to determine the nutritional grade and nutrition label for meals. If you have a little extra money to invest and do not have a smart phone, you can also buy a hand held device that is strictly a calorie calculator. Most look like small label makers. This is a great option for people who don't have constant access to the internet, or who may travel a lot.

If you are new to blending foods remember that ample liquid is a key part to mixing. Liquid gives the mix the fluidity it needs to break the food down and blend a smoother mix.

Remember, it is not advisable to use hard boiled or hard scrambled eggs. The consistency is usually grainy and clogs easily in the tube. The recipe I have for eggs has a small grainy look to it once pureed but thinned down works very well as a protein base and goes great with just about anything you can think of to mix with it.

To test your new recipes, keep one of your child's old feeding tubes you would normally discard after the 1-7 days of use. This will be a valuable tool for some foods that maybe are very fine but not fine enough to fit through the mesh strainer. Try pushing 5 mL through the tube to see if it will make it all the way through. If you can get small and not completely broken down protein into your child, it will satisfy their stomach and stabilize their blood sugar more successfully.

NEVER force food through that may seem stuck. Go through your regular routine to determine where the plug has occurred. If it is in the button, use the special tool that came with your kit to open it back up. I used 1 mL of air as a solution once, but only on an empty stomach. Again, this is why it is a requirement to strain and do trial runs on all foods that you make prior to feeding it to your child.

NEVER put extremely cold or mildly to extremely hot foods through the g-tube system. You could severely hurt your child. Always try to serve lukewarm or even room temperature foods. If you need to take a little of the chill off the food to make it more fluid, heat it as you would a baby bottle. Put the food in a zip locked bag and seal the bag.

Place the bag in a bowl or glass of warm water.
Allow it to sit for 10-15 minutes. Mix to
distribute even temperature and serve.

Remember that with the right attitude this can
be fun, if you let it!

AB & J

What kid doesn't love a nut butter and jelly sandwich? This twist on a favorite is sure to please.

Ingredients:

- 1 Tablespoon Almond Butter

- 1/2 to 1 cup Unsweetened Almond Milk

- 1 Banana or pureed fruit of your choice

Blend almond butter with 1/2 cup of almond milk in food processor until smooth. Mash banana with fork or potato masher, add to mixture. Add more milk in small measured quantities until desired thinning occurs. Juice may be considered in place of milk if concern of constipation arises.

Tip: When using a banana in any meal, mash it up with a potato masher or fork before putting it into the food processer. It will improve the blending of ingredients without having to water down the mix too much or over blending decreasing the calories.

Greek Yogurt Morning

Here is a great tasting, protein filled breakfast that is quick and easy.

Ingredients:

- 1 banana

- 1/4 cup plain Greek yogurt

- 1/2 to 1 cup unsweetened Almond Milk

Mash banana with potato masher and put into food processor. Add Greek yogurt and 1/2 cup almond milk. Blend until smooth. Add extra almond milk until desired thinning occurs.

Tip: Add extra nutrition and great flavor by mixing a super food powder or baby food powder to this meal. Create an extra boost of calories without excessive volume added.

Eggs for Any Meal

Some may see the word custard and think a lot of skill is needed. Not true. Any level of cooking experience can make this work. Constant stirring at a moderate pace is needed to allow the eggs to cook without it becoming a solid mass. The key to this recipe is that the milk and eggs be the same temperature from start to finish.   Makes approximately 9 ounces

Ingredients:

- 1 and 1/2 cups to 2 cups Almond Milk

- 2 Large eggs

- 3 Egg yolks (Save extra egg whites for someone else to use in a morning scramble)

- 2 dashes cinnamon (optional)

Tools:

- Medium Whisk

- Frying pan or other large pan with high sides

- 2 bowls different sizes, metal or glass

- Ice

- Timer

Take bowls; place some ice in one with a little water. Place larger of the two bowls on the top to chill the bowl. Set aside.

Mix together all ingredients in pan. Next, turn on the burner between medium and low heat. Constantly whisk mixture over heat for 12-15 minutes. Mixture should start to produce little balls around the 12 minute mark. Once this starts to occur remove the pan from the heat. Continue to whisk for a few minutes as the mixture cools, then pour into chilled bowl. Keep the top bowl in the ice and water. Whisk the mixture on and off for 10-15 minutes to keep the mixture from clumping while it cools. Once the mixture is completely cooled down, put into food processor and blend until smooth. Place mix into refrigerator. Do not use until mixture has been completly chilled.

NEVER FEED HOT FOOD TO YOUR CHILD THROUGH THEIR TUBE AS YOU MAY BURN THEM SEVERELY

Tips: If you would like to use cow's milk ratio should be 2 cups milk to eggs and two egg yolks. Follow directions above.

To make a dessert for the rest of the family, add sugar to taste. Garnish with lemon or berries for an

 Egg-citing pudding alternative.

Simple Applesauce

This simple sauce is easy to make and is a crowd pleaser.

Ingredients:

- 4 or 5 Organic Apples

- water

- 1/4 teaspoon Cinnamon (optional to taste)

- 1/4 teaspoon nutmeg (optional)

Peel apples and cut into chunks. Place apples in saucepan. Put in enough water to almost cover apples. Add cinnamon and nutmeg. Put on medium heat until it starts to boil then turn down to a low simmer. Stir and mash with potato masher on and off until very soft. Take off the burner and let cool down. Place in storage container and put in fridge. The sauce should be slightly chunky. Once completely cooled applesauce can be pureed or served as is to non g-tube fed children.

NEVER FEED HOT FOOD TO YOUR CHILD THROUGH THEIR TUBE AS YOU MAY BURN THEM SEVERELY

Tip: Honey can be added to taste during cooking if age appropriate. Check with your doctor before use. Addition of honey to mix creates a thicker, creamier sauce. Honey is not ideal for the G-tube but the others will enjoy it.

Appendix

Useful Websites

Calorie and Nutritional Analyzer

www.caloriecounter.com

Free Membership

Natural Health Website

Dr. Jeffery Mercola

www.mercola.com

Free Membership

Books

The South Beach Diet

By Dr. Arthur Agatston

Available wherever books are sold

The Fungus Link by Doug Kaufmann

www.knowthecause.com

Free Membership to Website and Shows Online

Books are not free but worth the money

What to Do with Your Brain Injured Child

By Glenn Doman

www.iahp.org

Warning-Some consider the IAHP to be too extreme so be ready for criticism and possible resistance from traditional medical practitioners. Most of which do receive the majority of their information from the drug companies or research medical journals which facts are not verified.   My rebuttal to those people is, "If it is so bad, why is my child exceling where traditional therapies have failed?" And "Why is it so successful throughout the world?" Don't let that discourage you to decide for yourself what is best for your child.

Preferred Products

Here is a short list of my preferred products. This is not an endorsement. It is for reference purposes only should you like to learn more about these ingredients and find retailers near you.

Jarrow Extra Virgin Coconut Oil-Expeller Pressed

Baby's Jarro-Dophilus®

www.jarrow.com

MaraNatha: Butter All Natural No Stir Almond Creamy

www.maranathafoods.com

Trader Joe's Sunflower Seed Butter

www.traderjoes.com

Almond Breeze Unsweetened Almond Milk

Almond Breeze Almond & Coconut Milk Blend

www.almondbreeze.com

Beechnut Stage 1 Baby Foods for Meat Protein

www.beechnut.com

Fage Plain Greek Yogurt

www.fageusa.com

Kirkland Organic Chicken Broth

www.Costco.com

Organic Pacific Soups

www.pacificfoods.com

Look for coupons from some of these companies just for signing up for a free newsletter.

Made in the USA
Columbia, SC
17 June 2020